GET TO WORK!

FOLLOWING EXTREME WEATHER WITH A STORM CHASER

Gareth Stevens
PUBLISHING

BY JOAN STOLTMAN

Please visit our website, www.garethstevens.com. For a free color catalog of all our high-quality books, call toll free 1-800-542-2595 or fax 1-877-542-2596.

Cataloging-in-Publication Data

Names: Stoltman, Joan.
Title: Following extreme weather with a storm chaser / Joan Stoltman.
Description: New York : Gareth Stevens Publishing, 2019. | Series: Get to work! | Includes index.
Identifiers: ISBN 9781538212295 (pbk.) | ISBN 9781538212318 (library bound) | ISBN 9781538212301 (6 pack)
Subjects: LCSH: Severe storms–Juvenile literature. | Storm chasers–Juvenile literature.
Classification: LCC QC941.3 S7585 2019 | DDC 551.55–dc23

Published in 2019 by
Gareth Stevens Publishing
111 East 14th Street, Suite 349
New York, NY 10003

Designer: Bethany Perl
Editor: Joan Stoltman

Photo credits: Cover, pp. 1, 7 Jim Reed/Corbis Documentary/Getty Images; pp. 1-24 (background) MaLija/Shutterstock.com; pp. 1-24 (rectangular banner) punsayaporn/Shutterstock.com; p. 5 ESB Essentials/Shutterstock.com; pp. 8-18 (text box) LoveVectorGirl/Shutterstock.com; p. 9 Joe Raedle/ Getty Images News/Getty Images; p. 11 Chris Johns/National Geographic/Getty Images; p. 13 (inset) NOAA Photo Library/Sterling, Virginia WSFO/Flickr.com; p. 13 (main) NOAA Photo Library/ Dr. Mike Coniglio, NOAA NSSL/VORTEX II/Flickr.com; p. 15 NAN SKYBLACK/Shutterstock.com; p. 17 (both) Minerva Studio/Shutterstock.com; p. 18 ROBERT SULLIVAN/AFP/Getty Images; p. 19 Visions of America/Universal Images Group/Getty Images; p. 21 (background) siriwat wongchana/Shutterstock.com; p. 21 (tornado bottle) A Yee/Flickr.com; p. 21 (torn paper and tape) Flas100/Shutterstock.com.

CPSIA compliance information: Batch #CS18GS: For further information contact Gareth Stevens, New York, New York at 1-800-542-2595.

CONTENTS

Someone's Gotta Do It! 4

All About That Chase! 6

What Does It Take? 8

Time to Chase 10

Tools of the Trade 12

Terrible Tornado Tales 14

Why Chase Tornadoes? 16

Hurricane Hunting 18

Get to Work! 20

Glossary 22

For More Information 23

Index 24

Words in the glossary appear in **bold** type the first time they are used in the text.

SOMEONE'S GOTTA DO IT!

Most people stay inside—or even hide!—during storms. But storm chasers drive to see storms! These brave scientists drive thousands of miles year after year to observe storms in person so they can learn how they work.

Before 1950, little was known about how storms formed. There were no warnings for **tornadoes**, so no one had time to hide! Many people died. Now, we can warn people up to 14 minutes before a tornado hits. It's better than before, but still not enough time!

There are around 1,200 tornadoes in the United States every year, with an average of 60 deaths. Once storm chasers discover exactly what causes tornadoes, they can help stop some of these deaths!

5

ALL ABOUT THAT CHASE!

Storm chasing is a dangerous job. The deadliest part isn't the storm. It's being on the road near a storm! Storm chasers always have a driver who'll watch the road and truck, not the storm. Since tornadoes can appear from any direction—and even change directions!—drivers have to plan for quick escapes at any time.

Storm chasers never chase after dark or through heavy rain because they can't see safely. After all, they want to see a tornado, not be a part of it!

START A WEATHER NOTEBOOK!

Fill a new notebook with notes on the weather. Make a new page for each day. Keep track of what the news says the weather *will be*, as well as what the weather actually *is*. How often is your local news right?

Once storm chasers are close to a storm, there isn't time to eat, sleep, or go to the bathroom. The chase is on!

SEVERE WEATHER
RESEARCH UNIT #2

SKYWARN

EXPLORER

7

WHAT DOES IT TAKE?

The only people chasing storms should be meteorologists. Meteorologists are scientists who went to **college** for many years to learn about weather, air, storms, and forecasting, or telling what the weather will be. Many meteorology colleges even have awesome storm-chasing teams you can be on to gain **experience** with storms! These storm-chaser teams use only the top meteorology students, so study hard!

Even after years of college, you'll still study and read to keep up with all the new discoveries!

TALK TO A METEOROLOGIST!

Call your local TV station and ask to speak to the meteorologist. Ask them about college, their job, and when they knew they wanted to become a meteorologist!

The tools and trucks used in storm chasing cost a lot of money. A college will usually pay for those things for their storm-chasing team because it's part of their students' learning!

9

TIME TO CHASE

Storm chasers use their schooling, experience in storms, and lots of different tools to decide what storm to chase. Days before bad weather happens, they plan for hours using a lot of different kinds of **data**—wind direction models, wind strength charts, **temperature** maps, and much more.

Then, they drive. Almost 90 percent of storm chasing is driving. They might even drive 500 miles (805 km) in a day! Because storms can change quickly, they have to check and recheck their data the whole time they're on the road.

STUDY CLOUDS!

Use 3dgeography.co.uk/cloud-types-for-kids to learn about the different kinds of clouds. Add cloud notes to your daily weather notebook entries!

TV and radio meteorologists tell people what to do during a storm. When they announce a "watch," that means a storm is possible. When they announce a "warning," that means a storm has been spotted and people should quickly get to safety.

TOOLS OF THE TRADE

There are many different kinds of **software** and **hardware** specially made for forecasting. Some tools are used days before a storm, while others are used the day of a storm.

One of the most important tools storm chasers have today is Doppler radar. Radar is a way of using radio waves to see and find distant things. This tool can point to a tornado within a powerful storm called a supercell storm. Doppler on Wheels is a special truck that gets radar data by driving into the storm!

MEASURE RAIN!

Have an adult cut the top 4 inches (10 cm) off a 2-liter bottle. Using a **waterproof** marker and ruler, mark inches up the bottle with zero at the bottom. Place your bottle outside in a heavy flowerpot. Empty it every day, and record the rainfall amounts in your weather notebook!

DOPPLER RADAR

NATIONAL SEVERE STORMS LABORATORY

NORMAN, OK
WWW.NSSL.NOAA.GOV

NSSL 7

One kind of tool measures temperature, **pressure**, and **moisture** inside the storm. Storm chasers set them on the ground where they think a tornado's going to hit. These are often used in addition to the Doppler on Wheels, shown here.

13

TERRIBLE TORNADO TALES

Storm chasers know the best way to study tornadoes is to see them. They come from all over the world to a place called Tornado Alley to study these deadly storms! Many terrible tornadoes have happened in this part of the country.

In April 1991, Red Rock, Oklahoma, had a tornado with winds up to 280 miles (450 km) an hour. Scientists didn't even know tornado winds moved that fast! In April 2011, over 800 tornadoes hit several states—the most tornadoes ever recorded for one month!

TORNADO ALLEY, USA

MINNESOTA

WISCONSIN

SOUTH DAKOTA

NEBRASKA

IOWA

TORNADO ALLEY

UTAH

COLORADO

KANSAS

MISSOURI

ARIZONA

NEW MEXICO

OKLAHOMA

ARKANSAS

TEXAS

MEXICO

In spring, cool, dry air from the Rocky Mountains meets cold, Canadian air and warm, moist air from the Gulf of Mexico right over the top of Tornado Alley. This causes many supercell storms to form throughout spring and summer.

WHY CHASE TORNADOES?

So much about how tornadoes work is still a mystery. They can last seconds or an hour, though they're usually about 10 minutes long. That means storm chasers have to be in exactly the right place at the right time to study them!

Tornadoes are always formed by supercell storms, a kind of thunderstorm where the wind and air turn in a certain way. But not every supercell storm makes a tornado. Hopefully storm chasers will figure out why that is soon!

TIME A STORM!

Have an adult find an online video of a thunderstorm with sound. Write down the number of seconds between the lightning and thunder. Every 5 seconds that passes means the storm is 1 mile (1.6 km) away. How far away was the storm at the beginning of the video? At the end?

TORNADO

Lightning causes thunder, so they happen at the same time. But light moves faster than sound. Timing how long thunder takes to get to your ears after lightning tells how far away the lightning was.

HURRICANE HUNTING

Another kind of weather storm chasers study is **hurricanes**. Though a hurricane's high winds and flooding can kill, the deadliest part of a hurricane is the storm surge. The storm surge is a strong wave that hits lands and can be up to 50 miles (80 km) wide and 20 feet (6 m) tall. Storm surges cause 10 times more **damage** than a tornado!

The deadliest storm surge in the US was in Galveston, Texas, in 1900. Over 6,000 people died!

When hurricanes hit land, they can even cause tornadoes. In 2004, Hurricane Ivan caused 118 tornadoes in 3 days! Learning more about how hurricanes work will give people time to leave beaches and coastal areas and head to safety. This will save lives!

19

GET TO WORK!

There's so much we still don't know about storms! The world needs storm chasers who love learning and problem solving—and weather!

If storm chasing is for you, there are many awesome places you can work after college. You could teach and do research at a college. There are several government groups that study weather. The Storm Prediction Center in Oklahoma, the National Oceanic and Atmospheric Administration in Maryland, the National Center for Atmospheric Research in Colorado, and the National Weather Service all need smart scientists who love weather. Are you in?

A vortex is a mass of spinning air, liquid, or gas that pulls things into its center. A vortex appears here because the liquid is being pulled through a small space.

MAKE A TORNADO!

YOU'LL NEED

2 empty plastic soda bottles that are the same size (caps not needed)

water

a metal washer

waterproof tape

plastic bag that closes

DIRECTIONS

1. Fill one bottle halfway with water.
2. Place a washer on top of the bottle.
3. Turn the other bottle upside down.
4. Line up the openings of the bottles.
5. Seal the bottle openings together with tape.
6. Quickly turn the bottles over.
7. Holding the taped openings, move the bottles in a circle like you're stirring.
8. Soon a vortex will form, and water will spin from the top bottle to the bottom bottle!

LEVEL 2 Try out different motions—shaking, twirling, tipping it to one side.

LEVEL 3 Try different sized bottles.

LEVEL 4 Add several small objects to the water.

GLOSSARY

college: a school after high school

damage: harm. Also, to cause harm.

data: facts and figures

experience: a chance to gain skills by doing something

hardware: a tool used for a particular purpose

hurricane: a powerful storm that forms over water and causes heavy rainfall and high winds

moisture: water in the air

pressure: a force that pushes on something else

software: a computer program

temperature: how hot or cold something is

tornado: a damaging storm in which powerful winds move around a central point

waterproof: able to keep water out

FOR MORE INFORMATION

Books

Close, Edward. *Extreme Weather.* New York, NY: PowerKids Press, 2014.

Royston, Angela. *Storms.* New York, NY: Marshall Cavendish Benchmark, 2011.

Tieck, Sarah. *Storm Chasers.* Edina, MN: ABDO Publishing Co., 2012.

Websites

How Do You Make a Weather Satellite?
nws.noaa.gov/om/brochures/satelliteK_revA2.pdf
This online book explains one of the most important tools in storm chasing.

Storm Chaser
learner.org/interactives/weather/act_tornado/
Play this fun game about tracking a tornado in Tornado Alley!

Temperature
scied.ucar.edu/webweather/weather-ingredients/temperature
This simple game shows how temperature really works.

college 8, 9, 20

data 10, 12

Doppler on Wheels 12

Doppler radar 12

forecasting 8, 12

Galveston, Texas 18

hardware 12

Hurricane Ivan 19

hurricanes 18, 19

lightning 16, 17

meteorologists 8, 11

software 12

storm surge 18

supercell storm 12, 15, 16

thunder 16, 17

Tornado Alley 14, 15

tornadoes 4, 5, 6, 12, 14, 16, 18, 19

vortex 21

warning 11

watch 11